My Little GENEROUS GIFT

PETER PAUPER PRESS, INC.
Rye Brook, New York

PETER PAUPER PRESS

In 1928, at the age of twenty-two, Peter Beilenson began printing books on a small press in the basement of his parents' home in Larchmont, New York. Peter—and later, his wife, Edna—sought to create fine books that sold at "prices even a pauper could afford."

Today, still family owned and operated, Peter Pauper Press continues to honor our founders' legacy of quality, value, and fun for big kids and small kids alike.

Written by Hannah Beilenson
Designed by Heather Zschock

3 International Drive
Rye Brook, NY 10573 USA

Published in the UK and Europe by Peter Pauper Press, Inc.
c/o White Pebble International
Units 2-3, Spring Business Park
Stanbridge Road
Havant, Hampshire PO9 2GJ, UK

ISBN 978-1-4413-4209-6
Printed in China

7 6 5 4 3 2 1

OUR ACTIONS AND US

Have you ever tried something new? Shared a toy or snack? Given a hug or high five when someone needed it? Well, those are just a few examples of putting your feelings into action! And every action you take can make a change. You can make people smile and laugh, help others feel safe, and create something new for everyone to share. There's so much you can do, and there's no wrong place to start—so let's take action today!

One action is **Generosity**, and we'll meet someone who will help us learn more about it.

Hey, what's that?
It looks like a present!

That's right! I'm a **Generous Gift**. I can teach you about giving and generosity.

Generosity is when you share with others.

Oh! Like when I share
my toys?

Or when I share my favorite candy?

Yes, but you can share more than just things.
Really?

You can share your time.
How can you share *time*?

When you help out
with a chore,

or listen to a friend;

when you bake something for class,

or put your talents to use,
THANK YOU!

I think I get it—giving is when we think about what others need.

Exactly! Generosity is knowing that you're a part of something bigger than yourself.

You can be part of a family,

a group of friends,

even the whole world!

And we can all do our part to take care of each other.

Like how my parents take
care of me?

Yes. Generosity is something you can practice every day, and others can do the same for you!

I hope they know how much it means to me.
Why don't you tell them? You can write a note, give a gift,

or just say "thank you." That can mean a lot.

Okay, then thank **you**! You've taught us so much!

Meet My Generous Gift

My Generous Gift's name is:

....

I can share my:

....

....

....

I am thankful for:

....

....

....

....